Taking care of your

HAMSTER

A Young Pet Owner's Guide
by Helen Piers

Consulting Editor: Lucia Vriends-Parent

BARRON'S

First edition for the United States and Canada
published 1992 by Barron's Educational Series, Inc.
Text and illustrations copyright © Helen Piers 1992

First published in Great Britain in 1992 by
Frances Lincoln Limited, Apollo Works
5 Charlton Kings Road, London NW5 2SB

All inquiries should be addressed to:
Barron's Educational Series, Inc.
250 Wireless Boulevard
Hauppauge, NY 11788

Library of Congress Catalog Card No. 91-16035

International Standard Book No. 0-8120-4695-1

Library of Congress Cataloging-in-Publication Data
Piers. Helen.
    Taking care of your hamster / Helen Piers.
      p. cm.
    Includes index.
    Summary: Discusses how to choose, feed, tame, and take
care of a pet hamster.
    ISBN 0-8120-4695-1
    1. Golden hamsters as pets. [1. Hamsters.] I. Title.
SF459.H3P54   1992
636' .93233--dc20   91-16035
                        CIP
                        AC

Printed and bound in Hong Kong

4 5   9 8 7 6 5 4 3

Contents

Hamsters as pets

A fully grown hamster is about 4 inches long. It is mouse-like in shape, but plumper and sturdier. Its fur is soft and silky, and it has almost no tail.

Once tame, a hamster will let itself be handled and stroked without fear.

If you have never kept a pet before, a hamster is one of the best with which to start. Hamsters are gentle and good-tempered, and when handled kindly and patiently soon lose any fear of people, and become very tame.

If you decide to keep a hamster, you will need to buy or make a cage for it, but after that it will cost very little to feed and look after. Its cage will be easy to clean, and it will not take up much space.

Some people think that hamsters are not such good pets because they sleep most of the day, and are awake and busy at night when everybody else wants to sleep. But if a hamster is taken out and played with at the same time every evening or late afternoon, it will look forward to this, and begin to wake up earlier.

The hamsters kept as pets are usually *golden* hamsters. This species was thought extinct. Then in 1930 a female and her 12 babies were found in the Syrian desert. From this litter the first golden hamsters bred in captivity were born. Every pet golden hamster today is descended from that family.

Golden hamsters were originally all golden brown with creamy white on the underside of the body, the eyes large and black, and the ears gray or black. But now there are many other color varieties as well.

You can find white hamsters, cream, gray and all shades of brown, some the same color all over, others banded or patterned in two or more colors. Some have red or ruby eyes instead of black.

Their coats can vary too. The short velvety coated hamsters are called *satins*. There are also longhaired fluffy ones.

NOTE: If you want to keep *Russian* hamsters, read page 30, because they do need looking after a little differently.

Understanding hamsters

A hamster needs a nesting box where it can hide away and feel as safe as it would in its burrow under the ground. Some hamsters, however, are quite content building their own nest in a corner with hay or pine bedding.

To understand your hamster better, you need to know a little about how it would live if it were wild.

Golden hamsters come from hot desert lands, where they burrow under the ground to shelter from the heat of the sun during the daytime, and only come out to look for their food when it is cool in the evening. That is why your hamster sleeps during the day, and is awake and busy at night.

Food is hard to find in the desert. A wild hamster would travel far from its burrow, searching in the sand for seeds and the occasional green plant. Your pet hamster does not have to forage for its food but it still needs a lot of exercise. So it must have room in its cage to move about freely, an exercise wheel to run in, and perhaps a ladder to climb up and down.

During one night a hamster may travel as much as a mile or two just running in its wheel.

Wild hamsters hoard food when it is plentiful, in case of a shortage later. Hamsters have special cheek pouches into which they can stuff food and carry it back to a store in their burrow.

The instinct to hoard is still strong in a pet hamster. So, although you will be there to feed it regularly, your hamster will also use its cheek pouches and store food behind its nest.

Golden hamsters are solitary — each one living alone in its own burrow, which it defends fiercely. That is why hamsters must be caged singly, or they will fight for ownership of the cage.

A hamster's cheek pouches can hold food weighing half as much as itself. Food taken into the pouches is carried to a safe place and hidden. Hamsters living wild in the desert would starve during a long dry spell if they did not have this instinct to store food.

Hamsters are rodents — animals that gnaw. Like other rodents, a hamster's teeth go on growing all its life. It must be given something hard to gnaw on and wear them down, or they will grow so long it can no longer eat.

Things you will need

A nesting box.

Coarse sawdust for the floor of the cage.

A block or a small branch of hardwood.

Food (see checklist).

One type of hamster cage.

A drip-feed water bottle is better than a bowl for water, as it keeps the water clean.

Heavy earthenware dishes are best, because they do not get knocked over easily.

An exercise wheel: this solid kind is better than one made of metal bars, in which the hamster might catch its foot.

Never

On the cage floor
Never use rock wool — the hamster may get tangled in its long strands.
Nesting materials
Never give newspaper — printing ink is poisonous. *Never* use cotton wool, knitting wool, or man-made fibers — they can cause a blockage in a hamster's stomach. And *never* use straw — it scratches the inside of the hamster's cheek pouches.
Wood for gnawing
Never give laburnum or evergreen wood — they are poisonous.
Never softwood — it splinters easily.
Never put anything made of thin plastic in the cage — if the hamster swallows bits, it cannot digest them.

Nesting materials
(see also checklist and *never* boxes.)

The cage

Remember

- Will the cage allow your hamster to take all the exercise it needs?
- Is it escape-proof?
- Is it safe from other pets?
- Is it well-ventilated?
- Is there a place in it where the hamster can build its nest and feel safe and private?

Pet stores stock various types of cages, or you may want to build your own. Your hamster is going to spend all its life in the cage you provide for it, so choose carefully.

How big should the cage be?

An average cage is about 19 x 9½ x 9½ inches. But the bigger the better. The ideal size would be 29½ x 16 x 16 inches.

Will the cage allow your hamster to have all the exercise it needs?

Hamsters are very active. They need to run, climb, and burrow. A smaller cage that has a shelf with a ladder up to it can be as good for the hamster, and more interesting than a larger one in which it can run about on one level only. Most cages include an exercise wheel. If not, you can buy one separately.

This homemade cage has been built of ⁵⁄₁₆ inch plywood lined with formica. Joints are made with glue and panel pins. The whole front slides open sideways and is made of rigid wire mesh so that enough air can get into the cage.

Instead of having a door, the whole top lifts off this cage, which is very useful when you are feeding or taming your hamster.

Is the cage escape-proof?

Hamsters are good at escaping. They can gnaw through soft wood and squeeze through narrow gaps. Be especially careful about this if you make your own cage.

Will your hamster be sheltered enough?

Your hamster will be more sheltered in a cage with a solid back and sides. However, these cages are not easy to find ready-made, so if your cage has bars all around, keep it tucked into a corner, out of drafts.

Nesting boxes

Your hamster will need a nesting box. You can buy one or make one out of hardwood. It should have a lid so that you can easily check whether your hamster is storing moldy food.

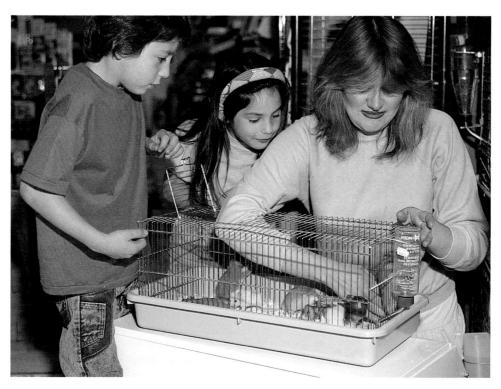

Try to buy your hamster in the afternoon when it is more lively. In the morning most of them will be sleepy. At the pet store several hamsters may be kept together. This is possible because they are still very young.

It is important to choose a healthy hamster. Ask if you can look at the one you choose outside its cage.

Buying a hamster

Your pet store will probably have a number of hamsters in stock, and you should take time choosing the one you like best.

What age should the hamster be?
It is best to buy your hamster when it is between four and seven weeks old, because it will be easier to tame when young.

Does it matter which sex the hamster is?
Male and female hamsters are equally good-tempered and easy to tame. But remember you can never keep two hamsters in one cage, because they will fight.

How can you tell if a hamster is healthy?
Its body should be smooth and well-rounded, not bony.

Its coat should be clean, particularly on the underside of the body, and with no bare patches.

Its ears should be clean inside, and, if it is young, covered with hair outside.

Its eyes should be bright and clean — not runny.

There should be no pimples on ears, nose, feet, or belly.

What food is the hamster used to?
Ask what food it has been eating, so you can give the same. If you want to feed it differently, wait a week or so, and then change to other foods gradually.

The pet store will give you a cardboard box in which to take your hamster home. But if your journey lasts longer than two hours it may nibble a way out. So take along a small wooden or plastic box. It must fasten securely and have air holes. Put hay and a little food on the bottom.

Taking the hamster home

If you have made your own cage, or bought one earlier, you can get it ready before you go out to buy your hamster.

Your hamster may be nervous after the journey, so instead of picking it up to put it in the cage, place its carrying box open on the floor of the cage, and let it come out to explore when it is ready.

Before getting your hamster, wash the cage with a few drops of mild disinfectant in water. *Rinse and dry it well.*

Cover the cage floor with a deep layer of sawdust and throw in a small heap of nesting material — hay, white paper, cotton material, and cardboard. Put a little in the nesting box to encourage your hamster to make its nest there.

Lastly, put some food in the cage and set up the drip-feed water bottle. Put in the gnawing wood, the exercise wheel and perhaps a cardboard roller for your hamster to play in.

When you reach home, settle your hamster into its cage as soon as possible.

It is not wise to play with your hamster right away. The journey could have been stressful for it, so leave it alone and quiet to explore its new home.

Where should the cage be kept?

Keep the cage indoors — it will be too cold outside. But never put it close to a window that gets hot afternoon sun, or by a radiator, or in a draft.

Remember to put the cage out of reach of cats. Although a cat cannot get in, it could frighten your hamster by trying to put its paw between the bars, or by sitting watching beside the cage, or even on top of it!

You will know your hamster is settling down happily in its new home when you see it beginning to make its nest or run in its wheel.

Feeding 1

Hamsters eat seeds, grains and nuts, vegetables, and a little fruit.

Hamster mix

Hamster mix is sold in pet stores. It is specially prepared to provide a hamster with a well-balanced diet of its essential foods — grains, seeds, and nuts.

Vegetables

Both root and green vegetables should be given, always raw.

Give fresh water every day.

broccoli

turnips

carrots

spinach

chicory

Some vegetables that are very good for your hamster.

How often should a hamster be fed?

Feed your hamster once a day, in the late afternoon or evening.

How much food does it need?

Give a small handful of hamster mix and a small handful of vegetables. If any is left uneaten, give less the next day. If all is eaten, try giving more, but first check that your hamster is not hoarding it in its cage!

parsley

outside leaves and stalk of cauliflower

After your hamster is 12 weeks old, you can give *small amounts only* of cabbage, Brussels sprouts and lettuce — but *not* iceberg lettuce.

Feeding 2

As occasional treats hamsters enjoy raisins, fruit cake, dog biscuits, sunflower seeds, and chopped hard-boiled egg. But be careful — too many sunflower seeds can cause skin troubles.

Extra vitamins

To make sure your hamster gets the vitamins it needs, you can buy vitamin drops for small animals at the pet store.

Water

Never leave your hamster without fresh water to drink. It is wrong to think it can go without because it is a desert animal. In the desert, hamsters drink the morning dew and find water in water-storing plants.

Fruit

You can feed pieces of apple, pear, grape, and tomato, all in small amounts only. But fruit decays quickly, and if a hamster eats bad fruit it will be ill. So check that none is left uneaten in the cage for more than a day.

When you want to go on vacation

If you are going away for more than three days, you must take your hamster with you, or arrange for a friend to feed it. For a shorter time — say the weekend — it is quite all right to leave enough food in the cage to last until you get back.

Wild plants

If you can recognize them, you can give dandelion, shepherd's purse, yarrow, chickweed, clover and groundsel leaves, and also *young* raspberry leaves (no prickly stalks). *But be careful! Many wild plants are poisonous.*

Never

Never give your hamster salted nuts, chips, chocolate, sweets, or anything sticky, which could get lodged in its cheek pouches.
Never gather wild plants from beside a road, because of pollution, and *never* from a lawn sprayed with insecticides.

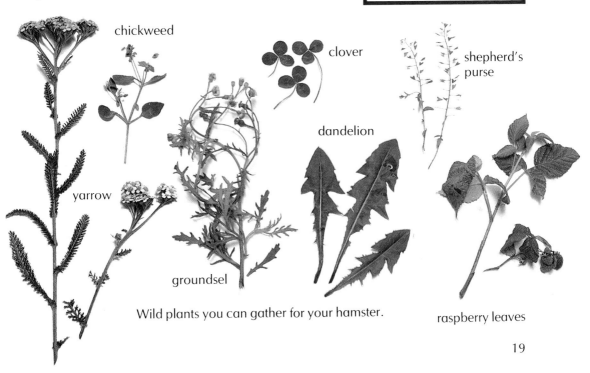

chickweed

clover

shepherd's purse

dandelion

yarrow

groundsel

Wild plants you can gather for your hamster.

raspberry leaves

19

Taming and handling

Before you handle your hamster you will need to tame it, which means overcoming its fear. You will enjoy doing this as long as you understand it will take time and patience. Do not put it off, because it will be easier while your hamster is still young.

Talk to your hamster all the time you are taming it. It will get to know your voice. Move your hands gently — they must seem large and frightening to a small animal.

You should be able to tame your hamster in less than three weeks, if you follow the described method. Do not rush it, or you may have to start all over again.

Do hamsters bite?

Only if they are frightened. A nip from a young hamster is not really painful, and not harmful. If your hamster does nip your finger, try not to frighten it more by jerking your hand away or screaming.

Never

Never wake your hamster if it is sleeping deeply.
Never shout or make sudden jerky movements.
Never pick up a hamster from behind — let it see your hand.
Never grip it tightly — let it run from one hand to the other.

Remember

- Play with your hamster at the same time every day.
- Speak to it softly all the time.
- Play with it for short times only, but often.
- Handle it over a table or near the ground, so that if you drop it, it does not have far to fall.

1. First watch your hamster for a few days to find out when it is awake and active — the best time to start taming. Note its favorite foods so you can use them to overcome its fear.

    Now start putting food straight on the cage floor, so your hamster gets used to your hand and learns that it brings food and means no harm. After a few days, leave your hand there while the hamster eats.

2. When your hamster is confident enough to eat beside your hand, put the food in the palm of your hand. It may be some time before the hamster will eat from your hand without fear. When it does, you can stroke it gently with one finger along its back, the way the fur grows. *Never* stroke its head.

3. Next, get your hamster used to being picked up. When it is eating from your hand, cup the other hand over it, and lift it gently a little way off the ground for a few moments at a time.

    After a few more days, if your hamster seems happy being lifted up, you can take it right out of the cage in your cupped hands.

4. Play with it over a table, letting it run from one hand to the other. Soon it will be confident enough to run along your arm.

Exercise and play

If you keep the hamster cage in your bedroom you will soon find out how busy your hamster is at night, digging in the sawdust and running in its wheel.

But for such an active animal, exercising inside its cage is not enough, and hamsters enjoy a daily playtime out of the cage.

Do not leave your hamster alone when it is out of its cage. You never know what it may get into. Some hamsters will climb anything, and hide in quite unexpected places!

An escape-proof play space can be made from hardboard or a large wooden crate with sides about 12 inches high, and sawdust in the bottom (for digging in).

Your hamster may be nervous at first and run to the nearest hiding place. But let it out every day, and it will soon grow confident.

You can put branches, boxes, cardboard tubes, flower pots, and other things in the play space to make it more interesting for your hamster.

If you decide to give your hamster the run of the room, first make sure it is escape-proof. There may be gaps between floor boards or under doors, which you never noticed before, but which your hamster will find at once. These must be blocked up.

Also make sure there is no electric wiring for your hamster to nibble and get a shock. And remember to check on the cat!

It is better not to give your hamster the run of the room until it is tame.

Letting your hamster out to play before it is tame

If your hamster is not yet tame enough to be picked up, put a small cardboard box on the cage floor. When your hamster runs into it, you can carry the box with the hamster inside to the play space.

Capturing a lost hamster

Try putting food in the cage, and leave it with the door open near where you think the hamster is hiding. During the night when hungry it will probably return and you will find it curled up in its nest in the morning.

Another way of recapturing a lost hamster is to make a ramp with a piece of wood up to a bucket in which you have put some food. When it is hungry, the hamster will run up the ramp and jump down into the bucket to get the food. It will not be able to climb out until you come for it.

Cleaning and grooming

If your hamster is to stay healthy, its cage must be kept clean, and never allowed to become damp.

Once a day

Take away leftover food, remove wet bedding, and replace with fresh material.

Once a week

Sweep out all sawdust or pine bedding and replace with fresh sawdust. Do not disturb the nest or food pile except to remove any food that is going bad.

Once a month

Clear out the whole cage, and nesting box. Wash it in soapy water with a few drops of mild disinfectant added. *Rinse and dry well* before putting in fresh bedding and nesting material.

Cleaning out the cage is not an unpleasant job if you do it often enough.

The nest and food store

Some hamsters get upset when these are removed. So perhaps when you clear out the nest, you could put back a little of the old nesting material to make it smell right. Then your hamster will not be too unhappy.

Longhaired hamsters need regular grooming to keep their coats in good condition. Use a soft toothbrush and be very gentle. Your hamster should enjoy it.

Hamsters are very flexible, and when they groom themselves they reach every part of their bodies.

Grooming

A shorthaired hamster will groom itself very well. If it gets very dirty, perhaps after hiding in some dusty corner, it can be brushed gently with a soft toothbrush. When really necessary, dampen the brush with warm water, but never let your hamster get too wet.

Health

If you think your hamster may be ill, do not put off taking it to a veterinarian, who will know if anything serious is the matter and what to do about it.

A hamster is usually healthy if it is fed correctly and given enough exercise, and its cage is kept clean, dry, and out of drafts. But even the best cared-for hamsters sometimes get ill.

How do you know when a hamster is ill?
It may refuse to eat.
It may sit huddled up, tired and sleepy.
It may have dirty, wet fur around its tail — a sign of diarrhea.
Its eyes or its nose may be runny.
Its fur may be dull.
There may be bare patches in its fur.

Ask the veterinarian to look at your hamster's teeth. A hamster's teeth go on growing all its life. If not worn down by constant gnawing, they may grow so long that it cannot eat.

What do you do if your hamster seems ill?
If you are at all worried, take your hamster to your veterinarian. Meanwhile make sure your hamster is warm and has plenty of fresh water.

On the next page are some of the more common illnesses and their symptoms.

Symptoms	Possible cause and what to do
Sneezing, sore eyes, and runny nose	This may be an *allergy*, perhaps to some nesting material, air freshener, or spray polish. But it could be a *cold*, so keep your hamster warm, and if no better the next day, **take it to the veterinarian**.
Fur around the tail is very dirty, and possibly wet	Your hamster has *diarrhea*, perhaps caused only by eating something that did not agree with it. But this could be the first sign of a serious illness called *wet tail*, so **take your hamster to the veterinarian at once**.
Bare patches in the fur	This may be just old age, or the hamster may have rubbed itself against something and worn the fur away. But if it is scratching the bare patches, they could be caused by *mites*. The veterinarian will give you something to clear them up.
Refusal to eat, a swollen cheek, and runny eyes	Your hamster has something stuck in its cheek pouch. **Take it to the veterinarian**.
After a fall, or being handled too much, the hamster lies quite still, as if dead	It is in a state of shock, though it may not be seriously hurt. If you leave it in a quiet, warm place, it should recover in an hour or two. **If not, take it to the veterinarian.**
Cuts — the hamster has cut itself on something sharp	Add a drop of antiseptic to warm water (boiled and allowed to cool), and bathe the cut gently. If it gets red and inflamed, **take your hamster to the veterinarian**.

27

Length of life

A hamster can live to be two or three years old, occasionally a little more.

But, however well looked after, hamsters sometimes die while still young, perhaps from an illness or after an accidental fall. It is always upsetting when a pet dies, but especially if you do not know the cause. So, if your hamster dies and you do not know why, talk to your veterinarian about it. He may be able to tell you what went wrong.

And, if you really enjoyed your hamster, do consider getting another to take its place. But of course you will need to clean and disinfect the cage thoroughly, along with everything in it, to make sure no infection is passed on to your new hamster.

Hibernation

Wild hamsters hibernate in winter when food is even more scarce than usual in the desert.

Pet hamsters rarely do this, but should you find your hamster curled up very tight, hardly seeming to breathe, and it has been allowed to become colder than usual, do not try to rouse it. Just put the cage in a warmer place, and it should wake up naturally in a few hours.

Never touch or try to pick up a hamster when it is sleeping deeply. Even if it is not hibernating, being woken this way will frighten it.

Unexpected babies

Breeding hamsters is best left to the professional breeders, because expert handling is needed to choose the right time for mating, and to prevent the male from being attacked and hurt by the female.

Also there is the very real problem of finding good homes for the young — as many as ten or more can be born in one litter.

It is very unlikely, but it just might happen that you buy a female hamster that is already pregnant. Hamster babies are born 16 days after mating.

You will know if your hamster does have some unexpected babies because you will hear their squeaks coming from the nest. **Do not disturb the cage to look at them**, or the mother may panic and attack them — her instinctive way of protecting them.

Hamsters are born quite helpless. They cannot see or hear, and they have no fur.

It is advisable to look for help on how to rear the babies in some of the books listed on page 31. Better still, consult your veterinarian.

Begin at once to look for homes for the babies, because when they are only five weeks old they must be housed separately or they will begin to fight.

You can tell which sex a hamster is by looking at its hindquarters, which in a male (*above*) taper towards the tail, but in a female (*below*) end in a shallow curve.

Russian hamsters

Russian hamsters are about 3 inches long, and can be recognized by the line of dark fur running from head to tail.

They are social animals, which in the wild live in family groups. So it is possible to keep more than one in the same cage.

If you want to keep Russian hamsters, you can follow the advice given for golden hamsters except for one or two points.

First, it is possible to keep more than one Russian hamster in the same cage without their quarreling. Even so, watch them carefully. When the females are pregnant, they can sometimes attack and hurt the males, and need to be kept in a separate cage.

Secondly, as they are half the size of golden hamsters make sure the bars of the cage are close enough, or they will escape.

Lastly, Russian hamsters need to be handled every day to stay tame, unlike golden hamsters, which once tame, will always be tame.

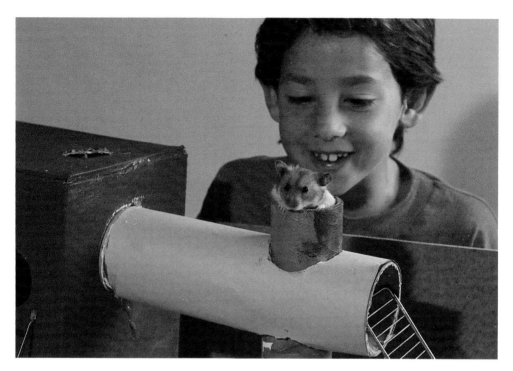

All through its life your hamster will depend on you for everything it needs. It will look to you for companionship as well as for its food, which it cannot go out and find for itself as it would if it was wild.

Your hamster will give you a lot of fun. In return do your best to keep it healthy and happy and make its life as interesting as possible.

Further reading

Hamsters and Gerbils
K. W. Smith
Bartholomew, London, 1976

Hamsters
Otto von Frisch
Barron's, Hauppauge, New York, 1991

Index